Pantomime

Marcel Marceau pantomimes sleep

Pantomime

THE SILENT THEATER

DOUGLAS AND KARI HUNT

ATHENEUM *1966* NEW YORK

to Karen

Contents

Illustrations

Preface

EVERYONE loves to play. When we are young, we play joyfully and with laughter. When we are older, we learn that play may be amusing but have a serious purpose.

We all start life by imitating those about us, and much of this imitation we call play. When boys imitate the adult world by building scale model airplanes, or girls by decorating doll houses, they are not only entertaining themselves, but are learning something about the world in which they must live.

The theater was created so that all mankind might play. By imitating life, the theater entertains us and teaches us something about the world in which we all must live.

The theater can reach our minds only through our

ears and our eyes. We may read the words of a play
using our eyes alone, but the theater does not really
come to life until we use both our eyes and our ears,
relegating words to our ears, and using our eyes to
follow the true language of the theater, pantomime, the
art of using the body to imitate life.

When and why did men begin to imitate life? How
can the language of the body speak to us even without
the help of words? Where has pantomime flourished
and what is its condition today? The answers to these
questions lie in the story of pantomime.

Pantomime

Balancing an elephant

*Balancing an elephant
with one finger*

LIONEL SHEPARD

LIONEL SHEPARD

Bacon frying in a pan.

LIONEL SHEPARD   *Matador*

What is Pantomime?

WORDS have been used for a long time as a means of communicating ideas from one person to another. But sometimes ideas are lost in transmission through words because people speak different languages, or because the same word does not really mean the same thing to two people. Languages continually change, and yesterday's words may not convey the same thought today. We are so used to words, floods of words, that we do not always realize that other things, music, paintings, and dance, for example, can also tell us a great deal. In the midst of our sea of words, we sometimes forget one means of communication that is more effective, more universal and timeless, than almost any other. It is as old as man, or even older, but as modern as television. This wordless communication is pantomime.

True pantomime is the transmission of an idea by movements and postures of the body. It is not the expression of words by bodily gestures, as in the game of charades, but the direct transmission of thoughts and feelings by means of the body alone.

The word *pantomime* is of course only a word and is not crystal clear the way a good pantomime should be. In ancient Greece, the word *mime* meant an imitator, that is an actor who imitated life in order to convey thoughts or emotions to an audience. Later, when the performances became broader and more spectacular, the word *pantomime* was formed by adding the word *pantos,* meaning *all,* to the word *mime.* This is somewhat similar to the recent creation of the trademark "Cinerama" from the word *cinema* to designate a wide-screen motion picture.

The words *mime* and *pantomime* are now used almost interchangeably to refer to the use of the body to communicate without words. *Pantomime* usually refers to the performance, and *mime* to the performer. Unless you know that the definition of the mime has narrowed down since ancient times, you may be puzzled to find out that the mimes in ancient Greece spoke. Ancient mimes were imitators of life. The modern mime is a silent imitator of life.

Pantomime, using the word in its modern sense, is the life-giving part of acting, just as oxygen is the life-giving part of the air about us. Pantomime is that which distinguishes acting from reading. An actor who speaks his lines but does not express what he says effectively with his body, is not really acting. Dancing in some cases is pantomime set to music. This is most evident in ballet and in ritual dancing.

Pantomime is sometimes used because the spoken word would be impossible. When a traffic officer on a busy street holds up his hand, it is not necessary for a driver to think of the word STOP before applying the brakes. The officer has used a pantomimic gesture because he could not be heard if he said STOP. He has said something with his body without words. Because for purely technical reasons there could be no sound, silent motion pictures developed their own style of pantomime.

But pantomime is not merely a part of acting and dancing, nor is it something to be used alone only when the spoken word cannot be heard. It is an art form in its own right, and has been presented as such from the time of the ancient Greeks and Romans to the present. When Marcel Marceau, the great modern mime, pantomimes the story of David and Goliath, he uses no sound because it is not necessary for a word to be spoken. The story is not only clear without words, it is communicated to the audience in a way that could not be duplicated with words nor added to by words.

Pantomime always deals with human emotions and reactions rather than with abstract ideas and reason. The scientific laws of gravity cannot be explained in pantomime, but a mime can convey to an audience the feeling of strain and effort involved in lifting a weight against the pull of gravity. When this identification with the performer is combined with the unexpected, comedy can be created. In a motion picture Charlie Chaplin once did a scene in which he was flying upside down in an airplane. Charlie did not know that he was upside down, although the audience did. When he opened his canteen to take a drink of water, the water seemed to him to fly upward, defying gravity. By pantomiming the reactions of a man unable to understand this sudden reversal of natural law, Chaplin created comedy.

More than most other performers, the pure mime stands alone. He receives no help from brilliant lines furnished for him by an author. He cannot rely on a melody furnished for him by a composer. He must use his own body and skill to communicate the desired emotional states to his audience. In the purest form of the art, he uses a bare minimum of costume, lighting, and stage properties so that nothing comes between him and his audience.

What, really, is pantomime? Because it requires no words itself, words cannot really describe it. But its history speaks for it in a way that descriptive words cannot.

The Earliest Pantomime

TO FIND THE earliest instance of pantomime, we have
to go back in time to a point before man made his
appearance. One evidence of this is the action of the
bee. A bee returning to the hive may be observed doing
a sort of dance on the surface of the honeycomb. This
dance has been studied and found to be a pantomime
to inform the stay-at-home bees about the location of
nectar, the direction in which it may be found, and its
approximate distance away. Another example of pantomime is the strutting of the peacock. He is not only
doing something that looks like the annual Mummers
Parade, but is performing a pantomime intended to
impress his prospective mate with his beauty and importance. There are many such examples, and in general all show that animals and insects use pantomime

to communicate on their own level. Since animals generally, and insects particularly, are very slow to change their habits, it seems safe to say that they were doing their own sort of pantomime long before the appearance of man.

After these primitive examples, the next pantomimist to appear is prehistoric man. It is not difficult to imagine Charley Cro-Magnon coming home from the hunt wanting to tell all his friends and relatives about the events of the day. Being more imaginative than a bee, he no doubt wanted to tell them not only about the location of the game, but also about how bravely he had pursued it, and how, in spite of his gallantry and skill, evil spirits had prevented him from bringing home any meat for the table. Lacking an adequate vocabulary to describe all this, he sometimes gestured and postured and invented dances and pantomimes. Primitive man was almost as slow at changing his habits as the bees, and we therefore have some of these primitive performances preserved as tribal rites.

Later, when primitive man began to think about the nature of things and to explain the things he could not understand through supernatural beings, he began to use pantomime and the dance to influence these gods and other creatures. On the walls of the caves of the Trois-Frères in Ariege, France, there are drawings of prehistoric men evidently performing a pantomime to influence animals, and possibly their gods. One drawing shows a prehistoric man in upright stance with the head of a bison and the tail of a horse. He is dancing, holding a musical instrument, before a group of animals. The conclusion is that he is performing a pantomimic dance to influence the animals and the gods.

Recalling the hunt

*Symbolic spirits of dead gods in a dance of the
Zuni Indians, performed to appease the gods*

Not having a highly developed sense of time, prehistoric man thought that he could reverse the order of things. If it was good to pantomime the successful hunt of the day, then he thought it equally good to pantomime a successful hunt when the hunting had been poor, in order to bring better luck the next day. These pantomimes were intended to influence nature.

The mythology of the Zuni Indians of the American Southwest includes a story of ten corn maidens who came from the underground regions with the remote ancestors of the Zunis. These corn maidens were given custody of the various types of corn raised by the tribe. They went into hiding, however, when threatened by the god of music, butterflies, and flowers, and it was necessary to get the help of the other gods to find them and restore the corn crop. A dramatization of this story, mostly in pantomime, used to be performed by the Zunis every four years, not to celebrate the event, but to bring rain for the corn crops. Rain ceremonies are still performed by the Indians of the Southwest, but the Indians are no longer primitive people, and the ceremonies are now done to influence tourists more than to influence nature.

Not all primitive pantomimes are religious or serious. Some are done purely for amusement. Such a performance is given by the Indians in the Aleutian Islands. The performers act out a pantomime in which they are hunters who see a beautiful bird and shoot it down from the sky. When the bird falls, it turns into a beautiful woman. This pantomime may be made up, at least partly, by wishful thinking.

Other primitive pantomimes tell the story of a legendary event in the history of a tribe. In some cases the event is real; in some cases it is mythical; and in some cases the event is basically real but the story has almost attained the stature of a myth by being elaborated and improved upon through the years. The Hopi Indians do a Serpent Dance, which tells the story of the struggle of the Hopis to survive when a great demon rose up from the earth and created a flood. The land sank, and the Hopis were forced to move on to other hunting grounds. Like most myths about natural catastrophes, this one is probably based on a real event. The demons and other characters were added to explain the disaster and make the story and the performance more interesting. It is more effective to pantomime a demon who causes floods than it is to pantomime a flood. A flood has very few human characteristics that can be imitated by a performer.

But these pantomimes, invented and performed all over the earth to celebrate, to amuse, and to influence the gods, were destined to become something more. Eventually, the most civilized of all ancient cultures developed, out of performances of this kind, the theater and pantomime in very much the same form as we know it today.

The Greek Theater

AT A VERY early stage in their history, long before
their Golden Age, the ancient Greeks performed ritual
pantomimes in honor of Dionysos, the God of Wine.
The celebration of the rites of Dionysos began in the
wild mountains of Thrace, where women called
Maenads danced frenziedly until they caught a wild
animal, tore it limb from limb, and ate it. It is from
the Maenads that we get our words *mania* and *maniac*.
Eventually the celebration spread to Greece, where
it became a procession to an altar for Dionysos, followed by a pantomimic dance around the altar, and
climaxed by the slaying of a goat.

The procession included a man representing Dionysos; men representing satyrs (woodland gods with goat-
like ears, pugnoses, short tails and budding horns);

16

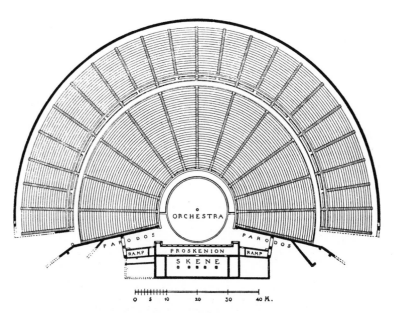

Plan of the Greek Theater at Epidaurus

The theater at Epidaurus, Greece

Dionysos, and Maenads, from a Greek vase

and girls carrying flowers and offerings for the gods. Dionysos was usually depicted as a middle-aged man, sometimes bearded, clothed in fawn skins, and wearing leaves and grapes in his curly hair. The satyrs who accompanied him were men wearing the tails of horses, who delighted in clowning, dancing, and pantomiming.

It is incredible that this ceremony should have evolved into our modern theater in all its variety, but it did. Alone among all the ancient peoples, the Greeks realized that the imitation of life could be used to make comments on life. Other primitive pantomimes have been forgotten, or are preserved only as quaint tribal rites for the amusements of tourists; but the festival of Dionysos grew into something more because it was used by men to say something to other men. The sacrificial slaying of a goat evolved into the performance of tragedy, which derives its name from the ancient Greek word for goat, *tragos*. The revels of the satyrs became comedy, from the Greek word for revels, *komos*. Because the original cast of the procession had included one principal performer, Dionysos, and a group of subordinate performers, the satyrs, the Greeks developed a style of performance in which a small number of principal players spoke lines and a chorus chanted, pantomimed, and danced. This style of performance is, of course, still popular in the musical theater.

The largest single step in the development of the theater was taken in Athens by Thespis, during the reign of Pisistratus the tyrant early in the sixth century B.C. Thespis was the first to set up a stage, put makeup and masks on his actors, and present performances that were more than festival celebrations. Actors are still sometimes called thespians in his honor.

Fortunately for Thespis and the theater, Pisistratus, although a tyrant, was very much interested in the arts and in things theatrical. When Pisistratus seized power in Athens, he hired a tall, beautiful girl to ride around the city dressed in golden armor, driving a chariot, after having spread the word that the goddess Athena approved of his taking over the government. The people of Athens saw the girl who was imitating Athena, and enough of them were convinced to make the seizure of power possible. Possessed of a sense of the dramatic, and a desire to increase the prestige of Athens, Pisistratus started a drama festival, and awarded a prize for the best performance. Thespis won the prize, a goat.

From then until late in the fifth century B.C., the theater developed at a rate never equaled before or since. In a little over a hundred years the theater advanced from semi-barbaric wine festivals to such plays as *Medea, Lysistrata, Oedipus,* and *Antigone* by such playwrights as Aeschylus, Euripides, Sophocles, and Aristophanes.

As Greek drama developed, Greek pantomime also developed. The two were inseparable because of Greek dramatic traditions that said that the number of speaking parts in a Greek tragedy could not be more than three. Therefore, it was necessary to portray all other characters in pantomime. This was really an advantage because, by the fifth century B.C., Greek theaters had become so large, that spoken words often could not be heard; and skillful pantomime was necessary to convey meaning to the vast audiences.

Some Greek theaters seated as many as 30,000 people and had a performing area almost 100 feet in diameter. Even to make it possible for the action to be seen, the Greeks had to develop a style of pantomime that utilized large masks and exaggerated costumes. The costumes, including platform-like shoes, were so unwieldy that it is thought that most of the pantomime was performed by the chorus, while the principal players stood still, or moved about slowly, reciting their lines.

Actually we know very little about the style of pantomime in the Greek theater. We know something of its rhythm since we know the rhythm of the words that were spoken by the chorus as they pantomimed. But we cannot see the pantomime itself. When we see Greek sculpture, we see something that has a colder and harder beauty than was intended by the sculptor. This is because most Greek sculpture was originally painted in lifelike colors. These colors have weathered away over the centuries. Just so with pantomime and the Greek theater. When we read Greek plays, we visualize something colder and harder than the original play because the element of pantomime is lacking. It became possible for people to preserve words when writing was invented; but the preservation of pantomime for later generations had to wait for the motion picture.

We do know that many of the techniques perfected in Greece have descended to us by a sort of evolutionary process. The wearing of masks to represent character types has persisted to the present and can be seen in the stylized makeup used by clowns, and by many modern pantomimists. There is an unbroken succession of slapstick comedians from the Greek comedy characters to the Three Stooges of today. The Greek mimes presented satirical plays to make fun of the customs, politicians, and dramas of the time. In the legitimate theater of our day, pantomime and satire are still trying to improve the customs, the politicians, and the dramas of a world that changes less rapidly than we sometimes think.

Not all Greek pantomime took place in formal performances of comedy and tragedy in the great theaters, however. Pantomime dances were performed by the soldiers of the city states of Greece, not merely as entertainment, but as training in control of the body and as training in discipline. From this beginning grew the military drills that have been used to teach discipline to soldiers for thousands of years.

There were also professional performers, mimes, singers, buffoons, magicians, and dancers, who worked wherever they could find an audience. They performed in villages, in cities, in theaters and outside; and after the decline of Athens as a political and military power they traveled over all Europe, bringing with them the Greek concept of theater: the imitation of life for the purpose of communicating ideas. Eventually they reached Rome.

Pantomime in Rome

ALTHOUGH the Greeks invented communication by means of body movement, their pantomime performers were seldom silent, but were usually either singing or speaking dialogue. The completely silent performance of pantomime was invented in Rome.

Greek comedy and tragedy were brought to Rome in 240 B.C. by Livius Andronicus, a Greek from Tarentum. At least this is what some historians tell us; although it is probable that other less noted Greek performers had been in Rome at an earlier date. The tradition is that Livius Andronicus lost his voice while he was performing for an enthusiastic Roman audience, and continued the performance entirely in pantomime. Finding that the audience was more enthusiastic about his silent performance than his spoken, he continued to

23

perform wordlessly. And thus originated the style of theatrical performance that was to become the most popular theatrical attraction in ancient Rome. This type of performance was given the name pantomime by the Romans, or possibly by Greeks who were then living in Italy.

The Romans became infatuated with pantomime. In the field of written drama they produced little of consequence, relying mainly on Greek importations; but pantomime suited them perfectly. During the next few centuries they produced literally thousands of skilled performers who acted out the stories of gods and goddesses: the labors of Hercules; the loves of Venus; the story of Mercury, the messenger of the gods; and the birth of Jupiter, father of all the gods. Some Roman mimes concentrated on comedy and satirized local affairs and even the gods and goddesses.

The Romans not only used Greek mythology as the basis for most of their pantomime plots, but also borrowed the Greek custom of the mask. They did make one modification however. The Greek masks had contained a trumpet-like device for amplifying the voice of the performer; but since the Romans had eliminated words from the pantomime, many of the Roman masks were made with closed mouths.

The Roman mimes possessed such technical skill that when they pantomimed boxing and wrestling matches, Romans came to see them in preference to the real boxing and wrestling matches. One Roman mime performed the story of Mars and Venus, playing all the parts himself, until it was said of him that he had only one body but many souls.

It was said by the satirist Lucian that the male mime

Greek and Roman actors—statues in stone

Greek and Roman actors—statues in bronze

must have the strength of Hercules, but the softness of Venus. He must know all the history of the world from chaos to the present. He must be so expert that each spectator of his performance sees himself in the pantomime as if in a mirror. He must be speechless, but be heard clearly by the audience; his hands must be tongues.

The description of a woman mime would be similar. The Romans had equally talented women who were mimes, from young girls to one female mime who was still performing at the age of one hundred and four.

It is possible that the Roman mimes were too skilfull for their own good. As time went by they tended to forget the Greek ideal of communicating ideas, and the Roman pantomime became entirely a demonstration of skill and spectacle. Roman audiences became more interested in personalities than in ideas. Bloody fights used to take place in the streets between the admirers of different popular performers, and even Caesar was unable to stop them. Instead of pursuing ideas, the mimes sought popular acclaim.

Although they sometimes made slaves of the mimes, the Roman Emperors were often admirers of the pantomime. Some of them even participated in the performances. The emperor Caligula once appeared naked in pantomime in order to give the people the opportunity to admire their emperor.

As time went by and the Empire became more affluent, the pantomimes became larger and more spectacular. The imitation of life vanished almost completely and the performances began to rely on spectacles of a type not seen before or since. Cavalry battles, elephant drills, fires, and even real executions sometimes took place.

While the formal Roman performances grew into great spectacles, small groups of less formal mimes continued to perform in the tradition of satire and buffoonery begun by the the Greek satyrs. Their satire was directed at almost everything, including Christianity. This, together with the spectacular and often vulgar entertainment in the Roman pantomimes, led to a great deal of friction with the leaders of the Church, most of whom denounced the mimes vehemently. It would have demanded an incredibly tolerant viewpoint on the part of the early Christians for them to have remained silent while the mimes burlesqued their religious ceremonies.

Although disapproval by the leaders of the Church is often given as the reason for the virtual disappearance of the theater in the fifth and sixth centuries A.D., it is more probable that the theater really collapsed because the Roman Empire collapsed. There are those who say that the theater disappeared because it was licentious; but the Roman talent for hydraulic engineering also disappeared, and very few would argue that the Roman aqueducts and piping systems fell apart because they were licentious. Theater on the scale of the ancient Roman pantomime requires a rich and highly organized society merely to build and maintain the structures required to house it. After the collapse of the Empire, such buildings were no longer built nor even maintained.

But although cavalry battles and Greek tragedy were no longer possible in the Roman theater, the Roman mimes continued to pantomime and juggle for audiences wherever they could find them. There was tragedy enough in the real world, and so the comedy mimes, wearing costumes of many colored patches, were still needed.

Medieval Entertainment

WHEN the Roman Emperor Diocletian divided the Roman Empire into the Empire of the West and the Empire of the East he little thought that he was creating a future home for Roman pantomime. Byzantium, the capital of the Empire of the East, later known as Constantinople, and still later as Istanbul, became the storehouse of Greek and Roman culture after Rome itself fell.

Byzantium showed little originality in the art of pantomime, but it did carry on the traditions begun by the Greeks and Romans, and kept them alive until the Renaissance. As in Rome, many mimes were slaves. And also as in Rome, the Church did not approve.

Despite continued opposition, pantomime now and then became a part of the Eastern Church. In the eighth century, Ignatius, a deacon of the Church of St. Sophia, wrote a play telling the story of Adam and Eve. Although the play has lines to be spoken, they were recited offstage by an expert speaker, and the action of the play was done entirely in pantomime. A hidden prompter beat time and gave cues to the pantomime performers so that their movements would exactly match the timing of the spoken narrative.

A similar technique, separating speaker and mime, had occasionally been used in the Roman pantomimes. It was evidently very successful, since many of the scholars in the Middle Ages thought that all the Roman pantomimes and plays had been performed in this way. The scholars were mistaken, but their belief shows the important position pantomime had in their thoughts.

While the theater managed to survive precariously in the Byzantine Empire, professional performances in the rest of Europe were reduced to a very elementary level. Small groups wandered from place to place and performed whenever they could find an audience. They performed in the streets, at fairs, in castles, and sometimes in monasteries and churches.

The entertainment provided by these itinerant performers was of two different types. The North European peoples contributed storytelling combined with musical accompaniment, and the more Southern peoples contributed the pantomime, dancing, and other visual entertainment. The first entertainment was mainly for the ear, and the second primarily for the eye.

The Church remained opposed to professional entertainers, although most of its denunciations were directed toward the entertainment of the mimes rather than toward the storytelling of the minstrels. It is perhaps fortunate that these denunciations occurred, since they provide us with one of our sources of information about the mimes and their survival through the Middle Ages. Very little else in the way of written records survives, since the period was not one in which much was written down. A great deal of the literature of the time consisted of the songs of the minstrels, which were passed on verbally from one performer to another.

Although there is little written description of the mime performances during the Middle Ages, there are many drawings and paintings of the mimes, or *jongleurs* as they came to be called. The multicolored costumes of the Roman mimes continued on into the Middle Ages as the patchwork costumes of the jongleurs. And just as the costumes retained their old characteristics, so did the style of the performance remain similar to that in Roman times, although on a much simpler level. The mimes no longer pantomimed stories from Greek mythology, for they would not have been understood. They probably pantomimed events of local interest, and in some cases we know they were reduced to doing animal imitations.

One feature of the medieval jongleur's costume was connected with a curious festival called the "Feast of the Fools." If you look at pictures of medieval jongleurs, or fools as they were sometimes called, you will see many of them represented wearing a headdress that looks like a cowl with donkey's ears.

In medieval times, the Church thought that the drama and pageantry of its services were quite enough to satisfy any desire of the people for theater. One element was lacking however—satirical comedy—which

Medieval jongleurs perform

The Court Jester

seems to satisfy a basic human need. In the Middle Ages this need proved to be so basic that some of the lower clergy and many of the people developed a form of burlesque religious service in which the solemn and beautiful ceremonies of the Church were turned into a pageant of fools. This ceremony turned everything topsy-turvy. Old shoes were used for incense, riotous songs were sung, masks were worn, the clergy put on fools' costumes, and as the high point of the festivities, a donkey was brought into the church.

The leaders of the Church, of course, denounced the performances, but it proved difficult to stamp them out. Driven from the churches, the Feast of the Fools continued in the market places and streets. Eventually the custom faded away, perpetuated only in the costume of the fools, as recorded by artists.

Some of the fools, seeking security, became official comedians to kings, princes, and nobles. In addition to clowning, pantomiming, and singing, many of these court fools served their masters in war. Their theatrical skills were used to spur on the soldiers or knights of their lords, and many of the fools also contributed their efforts in actual fighting.

In France, Tribaulet, a court fool at the time of Louis XII, fought in many military campaigns. Henry III of France had a court fool named Chicot who was killed by the sword while in the service of his king.

In England, Henry VIII and Queen Elizabeth I had court fools. James I had a court fool named Jeffrey Hudson. Jeffrey was a midget who was very belligerent despite his small size. He once challenged one of the nobles to a duel. Thinking it a joke, the noble came to the duel armed with a water pistol; but Jeffrey was not joking. He shot the noble dead.

The court fools live today only in the plays of Shakespeare and in medieval art. The fools had sought security by serving the nobles, but did not really find it, for the position of court fool did not long outlast the Middle Ages. While the court fools were entertaining the nobility, the entertainment of the common people was developing with aid from an unexpected source.

Mystery and Morality Plays

IN THE tenth century a remarkable thing happened. The Church, which had for so long opposed the imitation of life, began to use a kind of theater. In order to dramatize the stories of the Bible for the common people, most of whom were unable to read, the Church began presenting mystery plays. At first, these plays were very brief and were performed in the churches.

The mystery plays, which presented, mainly in speech, the stories of the Old and the New Testaments, soon began to expand in more than one direction. On the one hand, the field of this new theater was extended to include what we call miracle plays and morality plays: miracle plays dealt with the lives of the saints; and morality plays dealt with the problems of the common man and his contacts with abstract

37

qualities such as faith, hope, ignorance, and love. In another direction, unexpected by the Church, the mystery plays began to expand into comedy, pantomime, and spectacle, complete with costumes, sets, stages, and even masks.

It had quickly become evident to the performers of the mystery plays that, while virtue is admirable, the imitation of it is rather dull. Therefore they made Herod, the three shepherds always present in nativity scenes, Noah and his wife, and many other Biblical characters into pantomiming and joking comedy performers. The most popular stage setting of the time seems to have been the mouth of hell. Devils, complete with frightening costumes and masks, poured out of elaborate representations of the door to hell and clowned on stage and in the audience.

There is little doubt that the professional mimes lent their assistance to this reborn theater. There are records of payments to professional mimes for their assistance in the largely amateur performances of the mystery and miracle plays. This was only natural, since the performances required skill in pantomime; and the art of pantomime is not easily learned except by direct observation and instruction. They were probably responsible for many of the comic interludes, similar to those they had been performing in the market places.

The Church soon became disenchanted with its entry into the field of the theater, and the performances moved out of the churches and into the market places. There the plays were no longer under the control of the Church. In Europe the plays were then put on by the towns, and in England by the guilds, which were something like our labor unions. Sometimes, in England, each scene of a play would be performed by a different guild, which would build its own set on a wagon. The wagons would be moved from place to place in the town, repeating the performance in each place, so that a spectator could stand in one place and eventually see the whole play.

The religious plays of the tenth through the fifteenth centuries, although they were a strange mixture of elevated plot and low comedy, helped to revive the Greek invention of pantomime as a means of telling a story and conveying ideas while entertaining an audience.

In the fifteenth century, when Constantinople fell to the Turks, the Byzantine mimes fled from the city and spread out over Europe. In Italy the mixture of religious theater, Byzantine pantomime, and wandering jongleurs reacted to create a new form of theater, the Commedia dell' arte.

The Commedia dell' arte

THE COMMEDIA DELL' ARTE, also known as the Improvised Comedy, was a theater of actors rather than a theater of playwrights. The plots of the plays performed were usually simple and seldom written down, except for a bare outline. The actors, each of whom concentrated on playing one stock character during his career, performed by improvising dialogue and pantomime to suit the situations required by the plot. The rough outline of the plot was posted offstage and referred to by the actors before going on. This gave a great deal of spontaneity and spirit to the performances, although no two performances were ever identical.

This style of performance was better suited to comedy than to tragedy. The best comedy must be played with the audience as a participant in the show.

40

Timing is all important in comedy, and timing can be sensed better by a performer in contact with a particular audience than it can by an author who must necessarily work alone. The performer must play on the audience the way a musician plays on an instrument. Although this is true of all performing, it is particularly true of comedy. The Commedia dell' arte performances required actors of superb skill; but given them, it could and did succeed magnificently.

A typical performance might involve a romance between Arlecchino and Columbina. Pantalone, the father of Columbina, and his friend Il Dottore, try to trick Columbina into marrying Capitano; but Arlecchino and his partner Pedrolino outwit them. Other complications are introduced by characters satirizing the manners and morals of different cities, rural areas, and countries.

Arlecchino, better known to us now by his French name, Harlequin, was originally an amorous, stupid, and swindling servant. His varicolored costume was derived from the ancient Roman pantomime, and he wore a black half-mask. He had a lively bouncing style of pantomime that is thought to owe something to the demon figures in the mystery plays. In a way Harlequin was a magician; he always carried a magic wand with which he sometimes worked miracles.

A famous Commedia dell' arte player, Dominique, the favorite of King Louis XIV of France, later made Harlequin into a much more debonair and graceful character. Dominique's characterization is the one usually used as a basis for modern portrayals of Harlequin.

Pedrolino, or Pagliacco, was, along with Arlecchino,

one of the two principal *zanni* of the Commedia. He was originally a shrewd and clever servant, to provide a contrast with Arlecchino. In France he was called Pierrot and made immortal by a great performer named Debureau. In England he was called Clown, and took on much of the bouncing, rascally character of the original Arlecchino when he was made immortal by another great performer, Grimaldi. He lives on in circuses all over the Western world, as well as in the opera and ballet.

Columbina, or Columbine, was the female counterpart of Harlequin. She was usually the love interest in the plays, and like most of the other more serious characters in the Commedia, she wore no mask. The characters who played comedy, the *zanni*, always wore masks.

Pulcinello was a hook-nosed, humped-back, black-masked mixture of stupidity and guile, villainy and love. He still exists, still pantomiming, for his modern speech alone would not convey much to us. We know him as Punch, of the Punch and Judy show.

Pantalone, or El Magnifico, was a physically old, but sometimes childish, greedy, foolish, pantalooned and bearded man. He was usually accompanied by Il Dottore, the Doctor, a caricature of an intellectual. The Doctor, whose field might be either medicine or the law, was much given to talking in long Latin phrases, which were understood neither by his fellow characters nor the audience.

Capitano—who was also called Capitano Rinocerante, Capitano Spavento, Scaramuccia, Scaramouche, and many other things—was a boastful, cowardly military officer. He is thought to be the

Engraving of Pantaloon by Jacques Callot

Scapino.   Cap.ᵗ Zerbino

Pulliciniello.   Sig.ᵃ Lucretia.

Riciulina.   Metzetin

Commedia dell' arte engravings by Callot

theatrical descendant of Miles Gloriosus, a similar character in the Roman comedies of the playwright Plautus. Overtones of Capitano's satire were often directed at the Spanish, who exercised military control over much of Italy at the time of the Commedia dell' arte.

Hundreds of other stock characters were invented during the history of the Commedia dell' arte. Sometimes a particular character would last only as long as the actor who invented him, sometimes, as with Harlequin, the character persisted even to the present. Some of the actors became so wrapped up in the parts they played all through their working lives that they assumed the names of their character creations, as well as many of their characteristics, in private life.

The life of a Commedia dell' arte player was not easy. It was very difficult to develop the skill in pantomime and in speaking to play one part extemporaneously. It was even more difficult to act in this way with a group, all of whom were improvising. There were other hazards too. The nobles who came to the performances used to walk on stage uninvited and take part in the show. The common people used to come to the theater, or temporary stage in the market place, armed with vegetables to throw at the performers if they were not funny enough.

Of course the performers were not wholly unprepared. Each performer had a stock of set speeches, which he used when they fitted into the plot. Each performer had standard pantomime routines that he performed silently when the need arose. These routines were called *lazzi* and consisted of pantomiming such actions as the eating of a hatful of cherries, or the catching of a fly and eating it. There were also standard *lazzi* to express emotions such as fear or anger or sorrow.

The Commedia dell' arte brought new life to the theater and affected the technique of acting right up to the present day. Although it created no great plays, it influenced many playwrights. Molière, for example, was trained in a Commedia dell' arte company; he wrote such plays as *Le Malade Imaginaire,* and became one of the greatest playwrights in French history. His plays are still performed throughout the world.

When the Italian players of the Commedia reached England, they influenced even Shakespeare, and he, in turn, had an influence on the Commedia dell' arte.

English Pantomime

THERE ARE accounts of the Italian players of the Commedia dell' arte reaching London as early as 1527. By 1574 they had attained enough popularity to be denounced by the Church authorities.

Shakespeare saw and was influenced by the Commedia dell' arte. There is evidence of this in many of the characters in his comedies. Parolles in *All's Well That Ends Well* is really Capitano from the Commedia. There is also evidence in many plot situations and in the "seven ages of man" speech in *As You Like It*, in which Jacques refers to the "lean and slippered pantaloon." But the superb use of the English language by Shakespeare and his contemporaries made the improvised dialogue of the Commedia seem crude. So the Commedia dell' arte in England stopped talking and became pure pantomime.

Neither Shakespeare nor any other dramatist would have invented a plot as incredible as the story of the Commedia in England from that point on. By a series of small steps over a long period of time, the Commedia dell' arte became a curious entertainment known as the English Pantomime. Curious, because it became a mixture of Commedia dell' arte, dramatized fairy stories with poetic dialogue, elaborate stage settings and parades, slapstick comedy, musical comedy numbers, and trick boxes and illusions. Harlequin, Columbine, Pantaloon, and Scaramouche were joined by such unlikely associates as Mother Goose, Alfred the Great, the Fairy Queen, and Dr. Faustus. Performers flew around the stage and over the audience on wires. A standard character known as the "principal boy" was always played by a girl. In one pantomime, King Richard III was played by the Clown. In short, the English Pantomime could include almost anything, and it still does.

In its most characteristic form, the English Pantomime consisted of an elaborately staged story from a folk tale, fairy story, or children's story, ending in a transformation scene that introduced the characters of the Commedia dell' arte who performed slapstick comedy noisily but without words. If you can imagine a performance of *Peter Pan,* changing in the middle to a Mack Sennett Keystone Cop comedy, complete with a chase scene, you will have some idea of what the typical English Pantomime of the nineteenth century was like. To visualize it in the latter part of the century, you might imagine that the Macy's Thanksgiving Day Parade had been moved indoors and combined

Clown about to be lifted to stage with mechanical trap

Mother Goose

ENGLISH PANTOMIME

Grimaldi as Clown

Grimaldi as Bold Dragoon

ENGLISH PANTOMIME

with the foregoing.

The titles of some of the Pantomimes give an idea of the fantastic variety of the performances: "Harlequin and William Tell," "Harlequin and Mother Goose," "Harlequin and the World of Flowers," "Harlequin and the Steam Engine." Although most of the titles included the word *Harlequin,* it was sometimes almost lost in an unusually long title, for example; "This is the House That Jack Built; or, Harlequin Pussycat Where Have You Been, the Little Wee Dog and the Good Child's History of England." Sometimes the word Harlequin was omitted and sometimes this made for increased clarity in the title, as in: "Aladdin," "Jack and the Beanstalk," "Rodolph the Wolf; or Columbine Red Riding Hood," and "Hokee Pokee the Fiend of the Fungus Forest."

The latter part of the usual English Pantomime, the part derived from the Commedia dell' arte, was called the Harlequinade. In it, Harlequin, Clown, and Pantaloon, all of whom did the comedy pantomime, had little time for imitating and satirizing life as their predecessors in the Commedia had done. They were so busy doing mechanical tricks—jumping through windows, or going up and down through traps in the stage to make miraculous appearances or disappearances—that they had little time for anything other than gymnastic ability. A standard joke of the time was that there were performers in some of the pantomimes who had never met, because while one was going up to the stage, the other was going down.

Among the stage effects that dimmed the imitation of life were the mechanical wonders known as "transformations." These were devices by which a chaise lounge would be changed to a wheelbarrow, a cheese to a rat trap, or Squire Bugle to a Clown. Although some of these tricks sound like miracles, according to contemporary accounts many of them were crude, often failed, and were simply pushed offstage. Fortunately, the pantomime was occasionally saved from the sterile pursuit of mechanical novelty by the appearance of a great performer. Such a one was Joseph Grimaldi.

In Grimaldi's day the main set used for the Harlequinade represented a street with a row of shops. Grimaldi pantomiming the part of Clown, would harass the storekeepers while helping Harlequin to elope with Pantaloon's daughter, Columbine. At the same time, Grimaldi would steal hams from a butcher shop, after having taken the precaution of greasing the steps with a pound of butter. When the butcher ran out of the shop in pursuit of Grimaldi, he slid on the butter. Grimaldi would offer to shake hands with Pantaloon and then hand him a red hot stove poker. After putting a dog through the butcher's sausage machine, he would leave the shop with a string of sausages. Another dog would bark and the last sausage would wag like a dog's tail.

Grimaldi's pantomime of Clown as a charming rascal was so fine that this part of the Harlequinade became frozen, and subsequent Clowns had to pantomime the part in his style. His fame became so great that even now circus clowns are called "Joeys," after Grimaldi's first name.

After Grimaldi, the level of comedy in the English Pantomime dropped considerably. No other performer could equal his Clown. The Harlequinade sometimes became too acrobatic and violent in an effort to fill the vacuum left by Grimaldi's retirement.

As the quality of the comedy declined, the staging of the pantomimes became more and more elaborate. Elaborate staging reached a peak during the latter part of the nineteenth century at the Drury Lane Theater under Sir Augustus Harris. Harris sometimes had as many as four hundred people on stage for one scene; and his sets were awe-inspiring. One set for "Aladdin," represented a dismal swamp inhabited by demons which, by a rub of Aladdin's lamp, became a beautiful palace on a lake, complete with a bridge over which a long procession was making its way. Some of his sets were so large that he had to tear out the back wall of the theater to accommodate them; and some of the properties had to be hauled on stage by electric tramways.

But the public eventually becomes bored with magnificent sets and spectacular staging. The merely colossal is no substitute for inspired imitation of life. This boredom began to express itself in a critical attitude toward the best efforts of the set designers. In one scene Harris installed several tremendous red lobsters in the set for an underwater ballet. One of the gallery patrons called out, "Gus, you've BOILED the lobsters!"

Although the English Pantomime continued to prosper and is still staged in many places in England every Christmas season, it never again reached the complexity of staging attained by Harris, nor the heights of comic inventiveness and pantomime achieved by Grimaldi.

Clowns

ALTHOUGH it is fitting that the clowns of the modern circus are called "Joeys," after Joseph Grimaldi, continental European clowns also owe much to the traditions originated by Jean-Gaspard Debureau in Paris during the early nineteenth century. Debureau played the part of Pierrot, not as a complete rascal, but as a complex character representing the common man of France. Debureau introduced into the character of the clown a blend of comedy and tragedy, wisdom and foolishness, avarice and generosity. This is difficult to portray in the circus, but is easy to portray in a play or motion picture about the circus. Grimaldi painted his clown with bold broad strokes to create comedy in large theaters. Debureau performed in a small theater and could pantomime a more detailed picture of a

54

clown as a human being.

The technique of the circus clown is limited by the conditions under which he performs. The circus clown performs at a rather great distance from an audience, which completely surrounds him, and is distracted by constant activity on the part of performers, roustabouts, and candy butchers. It is natural for the circus clown to rely on acrobatics, costumes, and mechanical tricks, rather than on subtle gestures. And well done, this can be a part of the tradition of satire that has been part of pantomime since the time of the Greeks and Romans.

Grimaldi's successors copied his acrobatics and gags, but they did not have his inventiveness nor his skill at pantomime. No one could match him until late in the nineteenth century when the Fratellinis appeared. The Fratellini brothers came from a circus family, and their comedy relied on broad action and an expert sense of timing, which was most appropriate for the circus. They were in the Grimaldi tradition, but were fresh and inventive and were best in their own environment. Their closing bit, in which one of the brothers sang a song while the other two brothers set fire to his hat, sunk an axe in his head, and pumped water on him to put out the fire, was much more successful in the circus than on the music hall stage. It was broad enough to get attention in the circus, but not subtle enough for the theater.

One of the clowns of the twentieth century who did succeed in performing in both the music hall and the circus was Grock. Grock, whose career began while he was still a child, was at first an acrobatic clown. After years of successful performing with circuses, he tried his clown routine in a theater in Berlin; but the audience did not respond. Grock realized that the type of performance required for the theater is different from that required by the circus. He began to move away from broad comedy in the Grimaldi tradition and toward Debureau's type of performance, using the clown as a pantomime character whose actions comment on life.

Beethoven's Fifth Symphony is sometimes said to portray man's struggle against fate. Grock used music to portray man's struggle with fate, but in a vastly different way. When Grock sat down at the piano bench and found that the piano was too far away, he would struggle to push the piano closer to the bench. When he tried to flip his violin bow in the air and catch it as an exercise in dexterity before beginning to play, he would miss it and have to pick it up from the floor. When he retreated behind a screen to practise, the audience could see the bow flying up in the air above the screen. He returned to face the audience and missed again. Not until he became so flustered that he threw the bow in the air and caught it without thinking did he succeed. Like all good comedy, these actions were not only funny in themselves, they were satirical comments on man and his struggle to tame nature. Grock went on to become one of the great performers of the variety stage.

In the modern American circus there are many able clowns, including Lou Jacobs, Paul Wenzel, Otto Griebling, Paul Jung, and Freddie Freeman, but they are almost overwhelmed by the sheer size of the circus. Much of the clowning is done in what is called a clown promenade or walkaround, in which the clowns circle

*Clown Lou Jacobs and his miniature automobile are
stopped by midget policeman Billy Levenson*

Three clowns admire a dummy clown head

CLOWNS

CLOWNS   *Otto Griebling as Sad Sack Otto*

the arena while performing, just as the wagons of the English Mystery plays once circled the market place, so that each spectator might see a complete performance. Each clown performs some bit of business as he circles the arena: one has a heart that lights up like a neon sign when he sees a pretty girl; one drives an incredibly small sports car; one wears a trick costume that enables him to change from an old lady to a midget and back again; one runs along pursued by a stuffed tiger which is attached to him by a thin wire. But it is difficult to think of gags that can be done while walking in a parade, and there is a tendency for any successful idea to be repeated so often that it becomes a tradition.

The circus was saved from too much clown tradition in the 1940's by Emmett Kelly. The usual clown costume is descended from the vari-colored costume of the Roman mimes. Originally it was intended to symbolize rags, to imply that the clown was an impractical fellow who had difficulty getting along in the real world. A long evolutionary process resulted in vari-colored but elaborate costumes, reaching some sort of a peak when the Harlequin costumes of the English Pantomime were decorated with as many as fifty thousand spangled sequins. Kelly reverted to the original idea and wore a tramp's costume of actual rags. The usual clown makeup is a bright-colored pattern, which serves as a trademark for each clown. Kelly used makeup to match his ragged costume. He invented an intimate style of pantomime in, but almost independent of, the circus. He would beg peanuts from children and then break the shells with a huge hammer, completely annihilating the peanuts, then search pathetically for the meat among the debris. He would follow the seal act with a frying pan, hoping for one of the fish thrown by the trainer to his performers. In trying to tidy up Madison Square Garden with a broom between displays, he would work industriously, trying to sweep up the lights cast by the spotlights. In brief, he brought pathos and pantomime back to the circus; and audiences loved it, as they always have.

Kelly performed during the entire circus, wandering around the audience and through the performing area. He created a new style, but there would have been chaos if all the clowns had followed him. So most of them had to go on inventing routines and tricks in the conventional manner.

The clowns of the circus, year after year, modify old routines and tricks and invent new ones. Grimaldi himself would have loved the tricks created by Paul Jung, who is the type known as a "producing clown." Jung designs and creates his own routines and properties in addition to performing. Grimaldi put a dog in a machine and out came a string of sausages. In one of his routines Jung puts a full sized man in a reducing cabinet and a midget comes out.

This sort of illusion, if it is done entirely for comic effect, belongs in the field of the clown. If it is done in such a way as to amaze the audience and make them wonder how it is done, it belongs in the field of magic, and the performer must act accordingly.

Magicians

A GREAT magician, Robert Houdin, once said "a magician is an actor playing the part of a magician." He might have said "a magician is a mime playing the part of a magician," for magic has often been performed without words, but never without pantomime.

The pantomime required by a magician is extremely difficult. A mime must convey thoughts and emotions to his audience through action. A magician must pantomime one set of actions to convey ideas and emotions while he is at the same time secretly performing another set of actions. For example: if a magician performs a routine of producing coins by plucking them from the air, he must, by his pantomime, make it seem as though coins are present at various locations in the air and then pantomime picking them from the air. He must at the same time, since he is not a real magician, be stealing the coins from somewhere without this being either visible or understandable to the audience.

To illustrate his reliance on pantomime, one magician once performed this coin trick without using any coins at all. He pantomimed catching the coins and dropping them in a champagne bucket that he held in his left hand. His only concession to conventional trickery was to have an offstage assistant provide the sound of the coins falling into the bucket by dropping other coins into a similar bucket while standing near a microphone. No one in the audience noticed that the coins were missing.

The magician must not only pantomime to aid in creating illusion, but must, by pantomime and talk, create a character that will interest the audience, just like any other actor or mime. Many magicians learn to do the sleight of hand necessary to accomplish their tricks. Some of them learn to talk well, but very few learn to pantomime the part of a magician well. This is why there are so few good magicians.

Like pantomime itself, magic as a form of entertainment started in prehistoric times and has continued without interruption ever since. Like the English pantomime, magic had a period of trick boxes and over-elaborate stage sets during the eighteenth and early nineteenth centuries; but magic was restored to artistic simplicity by a French magician, Jean Eugene Robert Houdin. Houdin, from whom the great Houdini borrowed his name, is considered to be the father of modern magic; for he was the first to play a gentleman magician without elaborate stage properties, relying on his skill in sleight of hand, speech, and pantomime.

The first great American magician was Alexander Hermann, who created a character that became the public image of a magician for generations. Hermann, who came from a family of German magicians, created a character almost like a new Commedia dell' arte character: that of a magician called the Great Hermann. He, of course, wore no mask, but his pointed mustache and goatee became the standard symbol of a magician. Like a Commedia character, he could improvise, and performed magic on stage and off; he was always in character. He acted like a man who could do the impossible; and the public loved his creation of a debonair and dashing wizard. He imitated life, not as it is in its more tragic moments, nor even as it is in its comic moments, but as everyone would like it to be if they could do miracles.

The great magicians who have performed "illusions," the magician's term for a large trick, like making a lady float in the air, have even more need of pantomime than the great sleight of hand performers. When Howard Thurston, Harry Kellar, or Harry Blackstone, great illusionists all, floated a lady in the air, the effect on the audience was not merely caused by the trick itself. The trick could have been done without the magician present. It was done by mechanical devices and offstage assistants. The function of the magician in this type of a trick is to make the audience believe in him enough to forget reason for the moment and almost believe that he is holding the girl in the air by an exercise of will, or some other impossible force. The audience, of course, knows better; but most people also know that all theater is illusion and are willing to go along with any performer who is really skilled in speech and pantomime, as well as in deception.

Probably the greatest magician of recent times is a Welshman named Richard Pitchford, known professionally as Cardini. Cardini, working entirely in pantomime, creates the illusion of a slightly tipsy English gentleman to whom magical things happen. His skill at deception and pantomime is so great that he performs, not as though he is a magician doing magical things, but as though magical things happen to him, surprising him quite as much as the audience. He uses no elaborate equipment, or it would be better to say that he uses no equipment at all. Playing cards, cigarettes, and billiard balls appear quite magically in his hands, disappear, and take on a magical life of their own. Cardini is an example of pantomime at its best. Using a minimum of properties, he projects an emotion, that of amazement, to the audience, without using the spoken word at all.

Magic and the Commedia dell' arte have one thing in common. In both, the performer develops a stage character with a distinctive personality and plays that character through various plots. Each performer creates his own characterization and the pantomime to go with it. In the Far East, in China, on the other hand, theatrical custom requires that the characters, the costumes, and the pantomime gestures be learned in a traditional pattern, even down to the smallest detail. For this type of theater the performer must be highly skilled and even more highly trained, but at the expense of creativity.

The Peiping Opera

THE PEIPING OPERA, or Chinese classical theater, is
the peak of Chinese theatrical development. It is known
as the Peiping Opera because it started in its present
form when theatrical companies came to Peiping from
all over China in the eighteenth century to celebrate
the eightieth birthday of the Emperor Chien Lung.
Many of these troupes remained in Peiping and formed
the nucleus of the present Chinese theater, which still
flourishes both in Formosa and on the Communist
mainland.

The Chinese classical theater, in contrast to the
English Pantomime, uses no sets at all, and almost no
theatrical properties. It does excel in elaborate costum-
ing, pantomime of a stylized type, and a degree of perfection and precision in performance that is rarely

65

equaled in the West. To the Chinese, the music and singing are also excellent, but this is not a matter for Western ears to judge. Our tone scales and musical techniques are so much different that comparison is impossible.

The Chinese have managed to substitute ingenuity and pantomime, tempered with a sense of humor, for sets and stage properties. The only stage properties in common use are a few tables and chairs. As each actor enters, he tells the audience who he is supposed to be, and if it is necessary, where and when the action is taking place. To indicate walking through a door, he pantomimes a high step over a threshold. If an actor climbs on one of the tables or chairs, he is supposed to be invisible to the other actors on stage. Battles are acted out by teams of acrobats, who do not touch each other, but merely tumble about until the vanquished leave the stage. Travel over water is pantomimed by a boatman with a paddle, who, together with his passengers, sways and flexes his body to simulate the rocking of the boat.

All the pantomime gestures and postures are performed strictly in accordance with tradition, and the actors train long and arduously for their roles. There are fifty gestures with the sleeve to be learned, and even more gestures with the hand, twenty standard smiles, and hundreds of other standard movements that must be studied and performed with grace and precision.

Masks are worn only to represent animals. Facial makeup, so intricate that it almost amounts to a mask, is an essential part of the actor's characterization. The design and complexity of the facial makeup as well as

Character from the Peiping Opera

Characters from the Peiping Opera

its color signify the type of character that is being pantomimed. Simple designs are used for the good characters; complicated ones represent complex and villainous characters. Red makeup represents courage; blue represents cruelty. Young men are clean shaven; old men always wear beards.

At one time the stage hands wore black to indicate that they were invisible, and could move about the stage to arrange the tables, chairs, and properties during the action of the play. This custom is no longer followed, but lack of visibility is still sometimes indicated by carrying a candle on stage to indicate darkness in which the actors cannot see each other.

Chinese audiences are accustomed to the symbols used in their theater. When Chinese drama is performed in the Western world, however, it cannot really be appreciated unless the spectator has studied the symbols and traditions of the Chinese theater.

Our theater has conventions, too, and is probably as difficult for someone from the East as the Chinese theater is for us. In the Eastern theater, the carrying of a tasselled riding crop by a Chinese actor indicates that he is riding a horse; in the West, the wearing of glasses by an American actor may indicate that he is studious. Such symbols can be understood only by those who know them, but the realistic pantomime can be appreciated by people anywhere; for people are much the same all over the world, and an accurate imitation of life is recognized by everyone when it is performed in pantomime. The silent motion pictures demonstrated this when they used panomime to become the most popular entertainment the world had ever known.

Early Movie Pantomime

IN 1872 Leland Stanford, the governor of California, made a bet that began a chain of events that led to the greatest deluge of pantomime ever seen. Stanford bet $25,000 that a galloping horse has only one hoof on the ground at a time. To win the bet, he hired a photographer, Edward Muybridge, to make pictures of a horse galloping. Muybridge, in order to make a convincing photograph at the precise instant when the horse's hoof hit the ground, invented a process for taking a series of pictures at close time intervals.

Paris, then as now, was a center of art and controversy. When an argument over the authenticity of Muybridge's pictures broke out among the artists of Paris, Muybridge went there to demonstrate his work. In order to convince the skeptical French that the pic-

70

tures really showed the galloping of a horse, he projected them on a screen in sequence, using a device that had been invented by an ingenious Frenchman named Reynaud. The silent motion picture had been born.

The motion picture is to pantomime what the printed word is to the spoken word. For the first time in history it became possible to make a permanent record of pantomime, and to allow great numbers of people scattered in many places to enjoy one performance. One of the first sequences of pictures presented at the Musée Grévin in Paris by Reynaud was a pantomime by a clown. The ancient Greeks had equipped their clowns with masks so that they could be seen from afar by a large audience. Now the clown could be seen from afar or near, anytime, anywhere, as long as the room could be made dark.

In the very earliest motion pictures, the quality of the performance was of no importance at all. The mere fact that the pictures moved made them a sensation. The most famous men connected with the earliest history of the motion picture were not actors, but technicians and scientists. Edison, the brothers Lumière, LePrince, Dickson, and Friese Green all made contributions toward the technical perfection of the pictures that moved.

The first man to give theatrical form to the motion pictures was a French magician, George Méliès, who operated the Théâtre Robert Houdin in Paris. Méliès became interested in photography, bought equipment in England, and in 1896 was aiming the camera at anything available, just like everyone else. Looking at pictures he had taken at the Place de l'Opéra, he was amazed to see a bus suddenly change into a hearse. He realized at once what had happened. The camera had jammed and had had to be re-started. During the time the camera was not running, the bus had pulled away and the hearse had arrived.

Méliès began to make films of similar tricks for his theater. By using the stop-camera technique, he made his actors appear, disappear, and change from one person to another. Soon he discovered other camera tricks and began to expand his operations. He built a studio and made the first motion picture sets. He discovered how to make inanimate objects move by stopping the camera repeatedly and moving the object during the time the camera was not running. This is the same technique now used in making animated cartoons. During his career Méliès invented most of the photographic tricks used in the motion pictures to this day, in addition to making hundreds of short films, including the first science fiction film, "Voyage to the Moon," and the first filmed commercial, an ad for a brand of wine, in 1898.

Méliès, although a performer himself, never paid much attention to the imitation of life in his films. He was primarily interested in tricks and spectacular effects. He was an inventor, like those who had invented the camera and the projector. By camera tricks and tricks of set construction the mime could now do anything he could imagine. But it took time for the mimes to learn to use the Aladdin's lamp that Méliès had given them.

In 1903, Edison made the first American movie with a plot. The movie was a western, "The Great Train Robbery." Although this film did not contribute much to the art of imitating life, it made clear something that had not occurred to Méliès: the scope of the motion picture is almost unlimited. It is not always necessary to construct sets. The whole world can be used for a set.

The true art of the silent film, of course, is in the use of the unlimited scope and trickery of the camera in order to provide a stage on which pantomime can portray the human reaction to all the forces of life and of nature.

In the earliest days of the film, the acting was not always the best, even though attempts were made to secure the best talent. The pantomime in the early films was exaggerated more than necessary for several reasons. For one thing, many of the people who made the films had very little knowledge of pantomime. The natural tendency of most people who try something new is to try too hard. A novice golfer swings much harder than an expert. Even the most seasoned of professional performers was a novice when the films began. The pantomime technique that had developed for the stage was too broad for the camera. Emotional states on the stage were registered by sweeping gestures meant to be seen from the second balcony. The camera on the other hand was staring right into the face of the performer. In addition to this some performers felt insecure without spoken words to help clarify their pantomime. The overall result was a method of registering emotion that often overshot the mark by several hundred percent.

As always, comedy pantomime showed that it could adapt to changed circumstances more readily than tragic pantomime. The first film comedian was Fred

Ott, an employee of Thomas Edison, who appeared in a brief film pantomiming a sneeze.

After this, producers quickly discovered that the exaggeration, unlimited scope, and pace of the film lent themselves naturally to comedy. Chase scenes, which had been one of the comic features of the English Pantomime, were greatly expanded in the motion pictures. On stage, the chase had been limited, but in the movies the chase could take place through streets, over cliffs, over rooftops, under water, or anywhere the imagination of the producer desired. The most impossible comic catastrophes could befall the performers when the camera tricks devised by Méliès were added to all the things the stage had developed.

One of the earliest producers of comedy films was Mack Sennett, who discovered such great pantomime performers as Charlie Chaplin, Harry Langdon, Harold Lloyd, Buster Keaton, Mabel Normand, and Edgar Kennedy.

The Great "Silents"

MACK SENNETT's comedies were the Commedia dell' arte gone wild. He encouraged improvisation, and his players rose to the challenge. Almost anything was tried for a laugh, and the nature of the motion picture made it possible to edit out anything that did not bring the desired laugh. Sennett's actors were run over by automobiles, thrown into lakes, ponds, and oceans, set upon by dogs, and hit by flying custard pies, all for the sake of laughter.

Although Sennett hired the best talent that was available to him, the spirit of improvisation caught on even among employees with no previous theatrical experience. Hank Mann, a former sign painter, stole a courtroom scene by making a hangman's noose of his necktie, while he was on a jury. Del Lord, a stunt man,

75

poured soap on a Los Angeles street intersection when the police were not around so that he could skid a car through the intersection for a chase scene. When Ben Turpin's expression did not suit her idea of pantomimed astonishment, Mabel Normand borrowed a pie from one of the workmen on the set and threw it in Turpin's face.

Not all of this qualifies as great pantomime, but it did bring laughs, much as the slapstick comedy of the Greek mimes, the Roman mimes, the *zanni* of the Commedia dell' arte, and the red hot poker of Grimaldi had brought laughs.

Although the silent comedies showed tremendous vitality and inventiveness, it became clear after a time that their problem in the long run would be similar to the problem that plagued the English pantomime. Mechanical tricks are good for a time, but they require the addition of a master of pantomime to portray human reactions and pathos in order to become an art. And fortunately, the silent film did develop more than one master of pantomime. Among the performers who made the movie comedy an art were Charlie Chaplin, Buster Keaton, Harold Lloyd, Ben Turpin, and Harry Langdon.

Chaplin was discovered by Mack Sennett, who had seen Charlie in an English Music Hall sketch called "Mumming Birds" in England, and "A Night in an English Music Hall" when it played in the United States. After playing a variety of roles in Sennett's short comedies, Chaplin began to create a stock character of his own. The idea of wearing formal clothes may have been suggested to him by Max Linder, an early French film comedian, but Chaplin converted the

Harold Lloyd in "Safety Last"

Charlie Chaplin as "The Tramp"

SILENT FILM COMEDY

Laurel and Hardy in "Two Tars"

Buster Keaton as a boy performer

SILENT FILM COMEDY

formal clothes into a variation of the rags that had been one of the standard mime disguises since the time of the Greeks and Romans. With his oversize shoes, oversize pants, elegant but tattered coat, cane, and derby he was the very picture of the little man against the world. As Debureau had once made Pierrot into the symbol of the French average man, Chaplin made the tramp into a symbol of the common man in a hostile world.

Other comedians of his time got laughs, but Chaplin was a great clown. He realized that comic pantomime must convey to the audience the human reactions and emotions that go with a ridiculous situation in order to make a comment on life.

Buster Keaton, another great pantomimist, began his career in comedy as a small child. His father, a vaudeville performer, brought Buster on stage disguised as a bearded midget, mopped the stage with him, and then threw him into the audience. One of his great contributions to pantomime was the substitution of his own expressionless, deadpan, facial expression for the traditional mask or makeup of the mime. No matter what comic catastrophe occurred to him, the "Great Stone Face" registered no emotion. He was a living demonstration of the fact that the pantomime of the body is more necessary to comedy than the mimicry of the face.

Harold Lloyd's career in one respect was similar to that of Chaplin. Lloyd experimented with a variety of characterizations while he was working for both Mack Sennett and his chief competitor Hal Roach. Finally, Lloyd invented the pantomime character that was to make him rich and famous. His career differed from Chaplin's in that he did not begin life in poverty as Chaplin had. This may have had an influence on the comic character he devised, for his screen self became a well-scrubbed, well-dressed, All American Boy type, who resembled an eager bank clerk rather than a tramp. This type may not have had the universal appeal of Chaplin's tramp, but it suited America perfectly and made Lloyd the chief rival of Chaplin.

In his horn-rimmed glasses with no lenses and his straw hat, Lloyd portrayed the earnest and energetic young man in conflict with a mad world. His films included some of the most terrifyingly funny situations ever photographed. Falling out of windows, hanging from the minute hand of a disintegrating clock at the top of a tall building, driving madly through traffic via automobile, streetcar, and horse, Lloyd always remained eager and confident that right would triumph in the end.

Ben Turpin created a screen character who represented the ridiculous looking little man who moved about with the greatest of confidence in himself. In many of his films, Turpin satirized, not life itself, but the other actors who imitated life. His imitation of Eric von Stroheim playing the part of an arrogant Prussian officer was a classic bit of pantomime.

Harry Langdon played the part of a pale, baby-faced, childlike adult who was perpetually puzzled at the strange world he found about him. He was very successful and well loved when he projected this character on the screen.

Stan Laurel and Oliver Hardy were among the few great comedians of the silent screen who successfully bridged the gap to the talking pictures without losing their touch at pantomime. Stan Laurel was in the same English Music Hall sketch, "Mumming Birds," that brought Chaplin to the attention of Mack Sennett. Coming to Hollywood to play in Chaplin type comedies, Laurel did not really find his element until he teamed up with rotund Babe Hardy. They complemented each other perfectly. Laurel, in his childlike innocence, would blunder into trouble and Hardy, exasperated at Laurel's stupidity would blunderingly try to straighten out the situation. Delivering a trunk to a house with fantastically long front stairs, or digging a tunnel for a jail break only to come up in the warden's office, they were a great pantomimic pair.

All these men were comic mimes who created a theatrical character and played that character in pantomime to make some comment on the world around them. The comments they made were not always clear or recognized as comments either by their audiences or by the performers themselves. But they were effective comments, or they would not have made people laugh.

Laurel and Hardy once played a scene in a movie in which they were captured by gangsters who took them to a dock, intending to dispose of them by throwing them in the river. To weigh them down, the gangsters put their feet in large buckets and poured concrete in the buckets. The police arrived just as the concrete was set, and the gang fled, pursued by the police, leaving Laurel and Hardy teetering on the dock, their feet weighted by large rounded blobs of concrete. Like the clown dolls children play with at Christmas, they teetered and rocked back and forth on the edge of the dock, trying, in terror, to reach each other for support.

They rocked over almost horizontally, but their weighted feet kept them on the dock. They always came to an upright position until they finally succeeded in grasping each other for support. This changed them from two teetering but stable forms to a single form shaped like a dumbbell: their weighted feet at each end, and their clasped bodies in the middle. They immediately rolled off the dock into the river.

Did this say that we are insecure as individuals, but sometimes even more insecure when we join together in organizations for mutual support? Laurel and Hardy didn't explain. They merely did the pantomime, and the audience rocked with laughter. To explain comedy is to kill it. Perhaps each person laughed for his own individual reason. But no audience would laugh merely because two helpless men fell into a river. People laugh, not because they see something ridiculous, but because they realize they have seen a subtle comment on the ridiculous.

When talking motion pictures replaced silent movies, pantomimed comedy began to disappear from the screen. Chaplin, Lloyd, Laurel and Hardy, and others continued to make movies, and Chaplin even made silent movies well into the talking picture era; but the drama, spectacles, musicals, and wordy comedies prospered while pantomime comedy faded into the background.

Tragedy and Sound

As successful as pantomime comedies were, the silent motion pictures had difficulty in creating effective tragic pantomime. The pantomime techniques used on the stage for tragedy were too exaggerated for the camera. Photography is realistic and yet allows such freedom and unlimited vision that it is an art form unlike any other. And silent tragedy, although it had a few great moments, failed to use the advantages and was caught in the disadvantages.

The comic mimes were accustomed to a different kind of exaggeration, and the silent movies gave them greater freedom to display their art. The advent of sound reduced this freedom, but even in the talking pictures Harpo Marx, the silent Marx brother, could create a fantastic Commedia figure of a clown who wore a plug hat, a ropelike wig, and a tattered rain-coat, honked an old automobile horn instead of using his voice, stole silverware, chased blondes, and generally carried on like Grimaldi, or the original Arlecchino.

But Harpo was an exception. In general the silent pictures were kind to comedy and less kind to tragedy. The addition of sound harmed comedy and helped tragedy.

But even in the silent film era some specialists were able to use the freedom of the medium to create unforgettable tragic characters. Lon Chaney was such a specialist, in the field of pantomimed horror. He became an expert pantomimist while he was a child in order to communicate with his parents who were deaf mutes. He liked grotesque and horrible makeup and characters, and made such films as "The Phantom of the Opera," and "The Hunchback of Notre Dame." He was a perfectionist and was willing to endure any discomfort to create realistic characters who combined horror and pathos. He suffered for many years from the effect of the harness he wore to play the hunchback, Quasimodo, in "The Hunchback of Notre Dame." Chaney's makeup and the characters he created are still imitated, but have never been equaled. Creating twisted and pathetic characters, he found that the potential of the screen for exaggeration was not a hindrance but a help.

Working on silent movies, however, directors soon found that they could control their actors like marionettes. They did not have to be skilled in their craft. If an actor was supposed to look frightened and was unable to pantomime fright, the director could frighten him while he was being photographed. Also, by editing the film, the pantomime of an actor could be altered to suit the director. Imagine a movie shot of a man laughing. If it is followed by a picture of a clown, the audience gets one impression from the pantomimed laugh. If it is followed by the burning of Rome, the audience gets an entirely different impression from the same pantomime.

Looked at in this way, the addition of sound to the motion pictures merely added one more method of avoiding the use of skilled pantomime to communicate. When sound was first added to the pictures, the performers talked, sometimes too much. In attempting to transfer stage plays to the screen, the movie makers not only forgot about pantomime, but also forgot about the other things they had learned to use as a substitute for pantomime. Action and realistic photographic technique were sometimes pushed into the background along with pantomime while the actors merely talked.

There were of course many motion pictures in which the pantomimed imitation of life was both essential and excellent. The industry eventually learned that, in tragedy and serious drama it was necessary to underplay the imitation of life to produce the proper effect. But pantomime was only one part of the movies. The spoken word, sets, costumes, scenery, and photographic technique and skill in editing all battled for attention.

Only occasionally after sound would a comic mime gain control of a picture and use the medium to make comments on life. W. C. Fields was one who did. He made several pictures in which he used his own brand of satire. Mr. Fields, who had juggled and pantomimed his way through vaudeville and musical comedy, both

wrote and acted in several pictures, including "The
Bank Dick." Mr. Fields effectively directed his pictures,
too, as he had a habit of improvising as he went along,
and the director was never sure what would happen
next. Mr. Fields satirized anything that displeased him.
Having had an unhappy childhood, he had learned to
be displeased with almost everything. In "The Bank
Dick" he worked out his dislike of small children, bank
officials, accountants, relatives, high society, and other
people and things too numerous to mention.

But only an unusual personality like Fields or Chaplin could wrest control of his pictures away from business men and management committees who tried not
to satirize anyone, but to please everyone. These men
made some very good motion pictures but only a few
of their pictures tried to convey ideas to the audience.
Their pictures glossily imitated, not real life, but an
imaginary life that was instantly recognizable as
"Hollywood."

Television Pantomime

TELEVISION has repeated the history of the movies, but at an accelerated pace. Television, too, began with pictures of anything that moved. One early half-hour show actually consisted of a view of people walking down the sidewalk in New York at the rush hour, with an accompaniment of recorded music.

However, television soon began to live up to its name, which comes from a Latin word meaning "to see" and a Greek word meaning "from far off." Television is not so much a new form of entertainment, as a new way of seeing old forms of entertainment without the bother of traveling. It has, in its brief history, shown most of the entertainment ever conceived by the mind of man. It has run through most of Hollywood's output of movies, as well as vaudeville, drama, sports, discussions, the circus, radio soap opera, symphony concerts, singalongs, and even foreign movies.

Naturally pantomime has been part of all this. Every show that uses actors uses pantomime. Even the wrestling matches are a form of pantomime. Many comic mimes have been seen on television, and a few have done pure pantomime. Red Skelton frequently does pantomime sketches and many of the bits of business he uses to liven up his shows, such as closing a door on his thumb and pantomiming a frantic attempt to free the thumb, would have been prized *lazzi* in the Commedia dell' arte.

In the early days of television, Jimmy Savo, a veteran of vaudeville, night clubs, theater, and motion pictures sang "River Stay Away From My Door" with pantomime gestures to keep the river away. Jimmy could play the wistful lovable little man in an oversize collar and ragged suit in such a way that audiences laughed or cried, just as he wished.

Ernie Kovacs did several all pantomime shows in addition to inventing camera tricks that Méliès never thought of. Kovacs tilted the stage and the camera so that the set looked level on camera, then pantomimed the part of a man who was puzzled at the peculiar action of gravity under these circumstances.

Sid Caesar pantomimed a baby, a German U-boat commander, a lady getting up in the morning, and even a white-walled tire. He pantomimed pantomime by doing a satirical imitation of a silent movie. His producer once said that Sid was so good at pantomime that if he pantomimed a man wearing an overcoat, you could tell what color the overcoat was.

But as television grew, it came to resemble the motion pictures of the days when the movies tried to please everyone. It began to avoid imitating life itself and instead began to create its own style of performance, primarily an imitation of the Hollywood movie. The simple direct communication between artist and audience by means of the body, the imitation of life to communicate thoughts and emotions as invented by the Greeks seemed lost. But while television was being invented and developed, a fanatically honest man in Paris was developing the theory of the mime and laying the groundwork for a revival of the pure pantomime performance.

The Modern Mime

In 1923 Étienne Decroux, an orderly at the Beaujon Hospital in Paris, went to a theatrical school, the École du Vieux-Colombier, to study voice in order to become an orator. While he was at the school, he came in contact with pantomime and realized that the language of the body, the art of the mime, could be more eloquent than words. He changed his career and became the greatest exponent of pantomime the world has ever known. He loved pantomime; he practiced at pantomime; he thought about pantomime; wrote about pantomime; created pantomimes; and researched to perfect pantomime. He was not interested in achieving fame through his performances. He did not especially like audiences. His sole desire was to learn all he could about pantomime and teach others to work as hard as

90

he did in order to perfect the art of the mime.

He believes that pure pantomime, without scenery, costumes, or photography is the purest of all the arts. He thinks that a performer standing in front of scenery disappears like a camouflaged cannon in a forest. Costumes, he thinks, are like the shell of a turtle. The motion-picture actor is not an actor, but a monument to be photographed by clever cameramen.

Monsieur Decroux's performances are rare because he devotes his time to practice and teaching, but they are a delight to anyone lucky enough to see them. He can portray the seven ages of man while walking across the stage, starting as a baby at one side and ending in senility on the other side of the stage. He can pantomime a gladiator, an athlete, or a tree with equal ease.

But it is through his pupils that Decroux has had his greatest influence. One of his early pupils, who soon became his colleague, was Jean-Louis Barrault, who is now one of the greatest actors in France. Barrault has become one of the most versatile actors in the world, able to play Shakespeare, Molière, and musical comedy, as well as modern drama. No small part of his success is due to the perfect control he learned from pantomime.

A young man who devotes himself exclusively to pantomime first appeared in a pantomime created by Barrault, "Les Enfants du Paradis," acting the part of Harlequin. Since that beginning, Marcel Marceau has gone on to become the greatest living pure pantomimist. Performing, usually alone, on a bare stage with a minimum of properties, he has made modern audiences realize that the most ancient form of the theater is also the most modern.

Marcel Marceau first became interested in the mime through watching the silent motion pictures of Charlie Chaplin, Buster Keaton, and Harry Langdon. In his childhood, he loved to imitate the people he observed, and even worked out pantomimes in which he would imitate inanimate objects such as trees, or patterns of motion like the wind, or the waves of the sea. It was almost inevitable that he should become a pupil of Étienne Decroux, and he did. And as Decroux is the ideal teacher of the mime, so Marceau is the the ideal performer.

Although Marceau has created a mime character whom he calls Bip, he has not allowed this characterization to become as essential a part of his performances as the tramp character created by Chaplin was to Chaplin. Bip is rather loosely drawn as a character and can be used in many different ways. In addition to this Marceau in his public appearances performs many of what he calls pantomimes of style, without using his character Bip.

A good mime should be able to make the audience feel that the imaginary world that he creates by his art is real. When Marceau pantomimes a man walking against the wind, you feel the wind; when he pantomimes a man flying a kite, you can feel the pull of the wind on the kite. In his style pantomime, "The Cage," you can feel the existence of an invisible wall that hems him in on the stage. He breaks through the cage wall, only to find that he is still in a cage that exists outside the cage. When he pantomimes David and Goliath, although you know there is no one on stage but Marceau, you feel the presence of David and Goliath at the

Pantomime "The Mask Maker"
MARCEL MARCEAU

MARCEL MARCEAU
as "Bip"

LIONEL SHEPARD   *accompanied by Jimmie Gavin*

DIMITRI

SALVATORE GUIDA　　　*as Capitano from the Commedia dell' arte*

same time. As Marceau goes back and forth behind a screen, he changes from one character to the other, but so expertly that he seems to exist as both characters simultaneously.

A great mime must be able to make the audience feel the emotions of the characters he portrays. When Marceau does his style pantomime, "The Mask Maker," he pantomimes a maker of masks who tries on masks until he finds one that he cannot remove from his face. The masks are not real, but are pantomimed facial expressions. The mask he cannot remove is a smiling happy one. While the mask expresses joy, his body expresses the anguish the maskmaker feels at being unable to remove his smiling mask. It would be difficult to find a better example of the pantomime of the body, as Marceau expresses sorrow and anguish by using his body, not only without the assistance of facial mimicry, but in opposition to the expression of his face. The contrast makes the emotion of anguish all the more real to the audience.

Decroux's faith in pure pantomime has been justified. New mimes continually appear all over the world, some of them pupils of Decroux, some of them pupils of former pupils of Decroux, and some of them knowing little of Decroux.

A young Swiss mime, Dimitri, pantomimes different national types, Frenchmen, Germans, English, and Americans. An Israeli mime, Shai K. Ophir, demonstrates the way different people smoke cigarettes and pantomimes a near-sighted Spanish dancer.

In New York a young Sicilian-American mime, Salvatore Guida, has made a one man show of the Italian Comedy, playing the roles of Pierrot, Capitano, and

Arlecchino in pantomime and dance, with masks by Umberto Monaco. New mimes continually come forward to catch the attention of the public, among them Lionel Shepard, Alvin Epstein, Phil Bruns, Bernard Bragg, Tony Martinero, Ronny Davis.

Lionel Shepard is probably the foremost American pure pantomimist. Unlike most American mimes of an earlier era, he is well trained in the theater. He studied drama at Adelphi College, studied dancing with Martha Graham, acting with Phil Schrager and Morris Carnovsky, and pantomime with Marcel Marceau. Wearing the traditional white face makeup of the mime, he has succeeded in bringing back to modern pantomime the satiric comment on current affairs which the ancient Greeks first introduced into the art of the mime. Mr. Shepard's comments though are as modern as the hydrogen bomb. In fact one of his pantomimes concerns the hydrogen bomb. He has also concerned himself with such subjects as James Thurber's fable of recurrent war, "The Last Flower," the hundredth anniversary of the first billboard, and the "Jabberwock" by Lewis Carroll.

Thus we have traveled a full circle. From the mime of the ancient Greeks, which used the silent language of the body to make satiric comments on current affairs and to express emotions too deep for words, to the most modern form of the mime, which uses the silent language of the body to make satiric comments on current affairs and to express emotions too deep for words. Unlike spoken language, the language of the mime is as permanent and unchanging as man.

Try It Yourself

WOULD YOU like to try performing in pantomime? Although not everyone wants to be a professional performer, almost everyone can benefit from some study of pantomime. Just as we need to choose our words carefully, we need to use our bodies carefully so that they project the images we want others to see. Most girls and women would benefit more from a study of how to walk gracefully than they would from a new dress, hairdo, and shoes. Most men, when speaking in public, have as much trouble knowing what to do with their hands as they have with knowing what to do with their voices. Pantomime can not only communicate an emotion to others, but can affect your own emotions. If you practice at walking confidently, you will feel more confident.

The best way to learn pantomime is, of course, by studying with an expert mime as a teacher. Many drama schools have good teachers of pantomime, and many mimes conduct classes in pantomime. In New York City, Lionel Shepard, Mata and Hari, and Étienne Decroux himself conduct classes in pantomime.

But not all mimes have studied pantomime formally. Many comic mimes have learned their art through actual performance before the public. Buster Keaton, Red Skelton, and Harpo Marx all began to perform when very young, and perfected their art before audiences. If you start young enough, perform before enough audiences, and have enough talent and fortitude, you can become a great performer. Unfortunately this method of developing skill is becoming more and more difficult; the opportunities for live performances continually decrease, and the level of skill demanded of a new performer continually increases. At present it is not clear where the comic mimes of the future will gain their experience.

Between these two extremes, of formal study and of rough and tumble experience, a great deal can be done by anyone who wishes to develop some skill.

First of all, it is well to remember that pantomime is physical, and the mime must have excellent control of his body. In developing this, not only exercises in the mime, but sports, diet, and gymnastics are important. The sports which are most useful are those that develop bodily control, such as tennis, rather than ones that develop specific sets of muscles, such as weight lifting. Exercises are somewhat an individual problem, and the advice of a competent physical instructor should be followed. The sort of exercises required are ones that loosen up and give control over all the muscles of the body. Some mimes recommend yoga exercises to develop the bodily control essential to the performance of pantomime.

The mime, like the athlete, must have good coordination and control of his muscles. Unlike the athlete, though, the mime must have control over all the muscles of his body; the athlete specializes in a more limited but concentrated use of the body. The mime must be able to look like an athlete if necessary, but the athlete need not look like a mime, or even like an athlete, as long as he competes successfully.

In learning to pantomime, the performer first learns individual actions and gestures, just as in learning any other language he would learn individual words. Then he learns to put these individual bits together and tell a story or evoke an emotion from his audience, just as a writer puts words together to create a story or a word picture when he wishes to affect the emotions of his readers.

A vocabulary of pantomime can be built up by observing and imitating the way people move in different occupations and situations, the way people of different ages, sexes, nationalities, and types move, the way people use their feet, their hands, their arms, their heads, and all the rest of their bodies.

Begin by pantomiming some simple action, such as pulling on a rope or digging with a shovel. Observe and try the real action with a rope or a shovel; then imitate it by exaggerating just enough to make what you are doing clear to the audience. The action must be modified to make it clear. For example you must face the audience even although you are pantomiming pulling on a rope which stretches off to the side of the stage. Try pantomiming pulling on the rope easily, then hard, then very hard. Observe the difference in bodily attitude which accompanies different degrees of effort. When pulling easily the feet can be close together. As the effort increases, the leg opposite the direction of pull must be extended, and the knee toward the direction of pull must be flexed. The attitude of the shoulders is different when pulling hard than when pulling easily.

Watch the way a performer walks on stage. Before he has even begun to perform, you can sense whether or not he is truly professional. A good performer can, by merely walking on stage, convey to the audience the impression that he or she is in command of the situation. Notice the way people of different types walk. The hesitant step of the baby, the confident step of the youth, the waddle of the overweight, and the hesitant step of the very old. A good mime can simulate any of these walks and many others without moving from one spot on the stage.

In order to simulate various walks, the mime must learn to select and accentuate the body movements of various types of people, and of people in various states of health and mind. It is not enough to copy the real life action literally, it must be analyzed and subtly exaggerated and modified to communicate the desired feeling clearly to the audience. The mime makes us see clearly that which we normally see only dimly and over a long period of time in the real world.

There are of course standard pantomimic gestures, such as the finger to the lips for silence, or the hand on the forehead to express sorrow, but the mime must use these sparingly or his art will deteriorate. Above all, the mime must never convey to the audience the feeling that he has unfortunately lost his voice.

Remember when you are pantomiming the existence of a material object that isn't there, that inanimate objects have rigidity and cannot move about by themselves. For example, if you are pantomiming digging a hole with a shovel, and are grasping the shovel with both hands, the hands must act when you handle the shovel just as if the shovel were really there. This is obvious in theory, but difficult in practice. When Marcel Marceau does his pantomime "The Cage," the walls of the cage seem to be present as his hands explore them, although of course there is no wall there on the stage. Although his hands move about, and he moves about on the stage within his invisible cage, the walls of the cage remain fixed in space as he feels them with his hands. This makes the emotion of being unable to break through the wall even more real to the audience than it would be if there had been a real wall on the stage. It is bad enough to be unable to break through a real wall, but to be unable to break through an invisible wall is terrifying.

Skill in dancing bears some relation to skill in pantomime, although dancing and pantomime are by no means the same. Dancing is like poetry and pantomime is like prose. Pantomime, like prose, may have its own rhythm, but it is not a rhythm forced on it by a pattern of music, as in the dance. There are other differences too. When a male dancer lifts his partner in the air, he must maintain the illusion that dancers never strain nor perspire. When a mime lifts a non-existent object, he must seem to strain, even if he cannot perspire. The dance denies reality, the mime creates it out of nothing.

Practicing in front of a mirror can be of some help, but it is dangerous. You cannot be the performer and the audience at the same time. It is far better to work with someone who is also interested in learning mime. You can then watch each other and learn by teaching.

If you are working with a partner in practicing pantomime, you can make a game of it by letting each partner invent characters and situations for the other to pantomime. For practice these can be almost anything, but they should be based on things you have both observed. For example it would be all right to ask your partner to pantomime an excitable lion tamer teaching a cowardly lion to jump through a hoop, provided you have both seen excitable people, and have both seen lion tamers. It would be going too far to ask him to pantomime an Egyptian guide selling souvenirs to tourists, unless you are familiar with and have seen such things. The aim is to create pantomimes that audiences can understand; and you will find it better to invent new combinations of things you understand than to try to use the pantomime equivalent of large and poorly understood words.

After you have built up a vocabulary, you can invent stories to tell in pantomime. Remember that the best stories have something to tell beyond the bare outline of a plot. Don't let the idea you want to express be too obvious, but let it underlie all of your actions. The story itself of course must be clear, but can be as simple or as complex as you wish. Marcel Marceau has done stories as simple as the catching of a butterfly and as complex as the dramatization in pantomime of Nikolai Gogol's story "The Overcoat."

Whatever story or stories you choose, however, remember that pantomime always deals with the here and now. It is impossible to indicate in pantomime that an event will not happen until next Thursday, or happened six years ago. Because pantomime, or the mime as it is often now called, deals only with the present you can tell a story in a shorter time than it would take to tell it in spoken drama. Not being weighed down by elaborate sets and costumes, the mime can compress time to suit himself. But the story must be one that adapts to this technique.

Other techniques and methods of conveying meaning will come to you as you work. For example, in speaking, one can often emphasize a point by using a silent pause. Jack Benny is one of the great masters of this technique in comedy. In the same way a mime can make his language clearer by using the pause as well as the movement of the body. Imagine a mime who has stolen a ham, like Grimaldi, and slipped it into his coat. There is a tap on his shoulder by a police officer who has come up behind him without his knowledge. If the mime turns around, or runs away, the situation will not be as funny as if he simply freezes into a motionless posture. A pause, when used properly, gives the audience time to focus its attention. The timing of the pause can only be learned by experience before audiences. And so it is with other aspects of the pantomimed story.

As you practice and increase your skills, the scope of what you can do, and want to do, will widen. The mime should be able to assume any set of characteristics he wishes without regard to costume or sets. For this reason most mimes wear some sort of neutral costume, and the traditional white face makeup. You may want to develop something characteristic of you. Because he

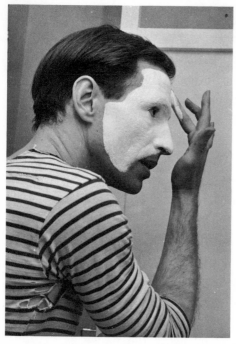

Applying clown white

Adding black liner

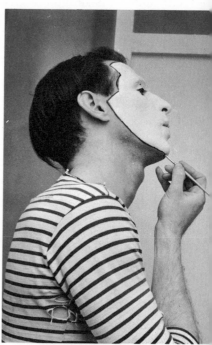

PUTTING ON WHITEFACE MAKEUP

Finished face

Applying lipstick

LIONEL SHEPARD

wears a costume which represents no particular style or time or place, Marcel Marceau is able to be David and Goliath at almost the same time on stage. Because he wears a simple black outfit and white face makeup, Lionel Shepard is able to appear on the same program as a soldier, a billposter, the first man, and the Jabberwock, without changing costumes. Whatever you choose should fit your style of pantomime.

Mime is an individual thing. Learn what you can from others. Then go on and invent the things that appeal to you.

Acknowledgements

Neither words nor pantomime are adequate to express our thanks to all those who helped us in the preparation of this book. Writing is a solitary and lonely business, but the accumulation of thoughts and information to write about requires the cooperation, interest, and patience of many people. Among those who provided assistance were Lionel Shepard, Dimitri, Tony Tanner, Paul and Mary Ritts, Nina Savo, Marguerite McAneny, Salvatore Guida, Umberto Monaco, Ronald Wilford, Wycliffe McCracken, and many others.

Also the staffs of the Rutgers University Library, the Douglass College Library, the Princeton University Library, the Harvard University Library, McCarter Theater, the French Cultural Services, the New York Public Library, the New Brunswick, N. J. Public Library, and the Museum of Modern Art.

109

Bibliography

Agee, James. *Agee on Film.* New York: McDowell, Obolensky, 1958-1960

Alley, Rewi. *Peking Opera.* Peking: New World Press, 1957

Barrault, Jean-Louis. *The Theatre of Jean-Louis Barrault.* New York: Hill and Wang, 1959

Bergson, Henri and Meredith, George. *Comedy.* New York: Doubleday & Co., 1956

Broadbent, R. J. *History of Pantomime.* London: Kent & Co., 1901

Cahn, William. *The Laugh Makers.* New York: G. P. Putnam's Sons, 1957

Chambers, E. K. *The Mediaeval Stage.* London: Oxford Clarendon Press, 1903

Christopher, Milbourne. *Panorama of Magic.* New York: Dover Publications, 1962

111

Dorcy, Jean. *J'aime la Mime*. Lausanne, Switzerland: Rencontre, 1962

————. *The Mime*. New York: Robert Speller and Sons, Inc., 1961

Decroux, Etienne. *Paroles sur le Mime*. Paris: Gallimard, 1963

Disher, M. Wilson. *Clowns and Pantomimes*. Boston and New York: Houghton Mifflin Co., 1925

Duchartres, Pierre Louis. *Commedia Dell' Arte*. Paris: Editions d'art et Industrie, 1925

Ginner, Ruby. *The Revived Greek Dance*. London: Methuen and Co., 1944

Herrick, Marvin Theodore. *Italian Comedy in the Renaissance*. Urbana: University of Illinois Press, 1960

Hunningher, B. *The Origin of the Theater*. The Hague, Amsterdam: Martinusnijhoff, 1955

Hunt, Kari and Carlson, B. W. *Masks and Mask Makers*. Nashville, New York: Abingdon Press, 1961

Hutchinson, William M. *A Child's Book of the Theatre*. New York: Maxton Publishers, 1956

Keaton, Buster. *The Wonderful World of Slapstick*. Garden City, New York: Doubleday & Co., 1960

Kelly, Emmett with Kelly, F. Beverly. *Clown*. New York: Prentice-Hall, Inc., 1954

Kinney, Troy and Kinney, Margaret West. *The Dance*. New York: Frederick A. Stokes Co., 1924

Kirstein, Lincoln. *Dance*. New York: G. P. Putnam's Sons, 1935

Kitto, H. D. F. *The Greeks*. Harmonsworth Middlesex, England: Penguin Books, 1951

Komisarievsky, Fedor. *The Costume of the Theatre*. New York: Henry Holt and Co., 1932

Life Magazine. *The Movies.* Entire issue of Dec. 20, 1963. Vol. 55, No. 25

Lawson, Joan. *Mime.* New York: Pitman, 1957

Laban, Rudolf. *The Mastery of Movement.* London: Macdonald & Evans, 1960

McCabe, John. *Laurel and Hardy.* New York: Garden City: Doubleday, 1961

Mantzius, Karl. *History of Theatrical Art in Ancient and Modern Times.* New York: Peter Smith Inc., 1937

Marash, J. G. *Mime in Class and Theater.* London: George C. Harrap & Co. Ltd., 1950

Marriott, J. W. *The Theatre.* London: George G. Harrap & Co. Ltd., 1948

Mawer, Irene. *The Art of Mime.* London: Methuen and Co. Ltd., 1955

Mills, Dorothy. *The Middle Ages.* New York: G. P. Putnam's Sons, 1935

Montgomery, John. *Comedy Films.* London: George Allen and Unwin Ltd., 1954

Mulholland, John. *Story of Magic.* New York: Loring and Mussey, 1935

Newton, Douglas. *Clowns.* New York: Franklin Watts, 1957

Nicoll, Allardyce. *Development of the Theater.* New York: Harcourt Brace, 1937

———. *Masks, Mimes, and Miracles.* New York: Harcourt Brace, 1931

Niklaus, Thelma. *Harlequin.* New York: G. Braziller, 1956

Nilsen, Vladimir. *The Cinema as a Graphic Art.* New York: Hill and Wang, 1959

Richy, Pierre and de Mairaige, J. C. *Initiation au Mime*. Paris: L'Amicale, 1960

Sadoul, Georges. *Conquete du Cinema*. Paris: Librairie Gedalge, 1960

————. *Georges Méliès*. Paris: Editions Seghers, 1961

Sennett, Mack. *King of Comedy*. New York: Doubleday, 1954

Strenkovsky, Serge. *The Art of Make-up*. New York: E. P. Dutton & Co., 1937

Taylor, Deems. *A Pictorial History of the Movies*. New York: Simon & Schuster, 1943

Tunison, Joseph S. *Dramatic Traditions of the Dark Ages*. Chicago: University of Chicago Press, 1907

Tyler, Parker. *Chaplin, the Last of the Clowns*. New York: Vanguard Press, 1948

von Pawlikowski-Cholewa, Harald. *Marcel Marceau*. Hamburg: Johannes-Maria Hoeppner, 1955

Wilson, A. E. *The Story of Pantomime*. London: Home and Van Thal, 1949

Douglas Hunt

is by education a mechanical engineer with a degree from Rutgers University, and by avocation a prestidigitator (magic tricks) and a photographer. His photographic illustrations appeared in *Masks and Mask Makers,* a book co-authored by his wife and Bernice Wells Carlson in 1961. *Pantomime* is a joint effort of writing, research and pictures for the Hunts.

Kari Hunt

has been a mask maker since 1946 when she began to create the masks for the television show Masquerade Party and television commercials. She attended Mt. Holyoke College, studied drama at Buffalo and Cornell Universities and studied mask making with Doane Powell. She has appeared on television with Ernie Kovacs, Jinx Falkenburg and others, and lectures widely on masks and pantomime in schools and clubs.